GRANDDAD YOU HAVE A MESSAGE III

Messages From The Universe

Granddad You Have A Message III - Messages From The Universe
By Alec Laidler

Published 2020 by Sazmick Books
Web: www.sazmickbookdesign.co.uk

British Library Cataloguing-in Publication Data.
A catalogue record for this book is available from the British Library.

ISBN: 9781912400409

Printed and bound in the UK using sustainable resources

GRANDDAD YOU HAVE A MESSAGE III

Messages From The Universe

SAZMICK BOOKS

ALEC LAIDLER

DEDICATIONS

I am dedicating this book to everyone who finds themselves on their spiritual journey.

Love and Light Alec.

CONTENTS

FOREWORD

In 2016, and since writing *Through The Eyes Of A Child*, I have moved from the Midlands to the Isle of Angelsey, North Wales, UK. This move, although physically has taken me away from family and friends, has helped me to further discover my spiritual self; who and what I truly am. I feel I have now reached my earthly home.

I hope you enjoy reading this book and that in someway it helps you on your journey of self-discovery.

Love & Light.

Alec.

INTRODUCTION

Having already written two inspirational books I thought this time on the earth is an appropiate to write a third book. My hope for you is that the book gives you enjoyment, enlightenment and food for thought at this time in your life.

Love and Light. Alec.

ABOUT THE AUTHOR

I originated from Co Durham in the Northeast of England and spent my early life there. Most of my life I spent in the Financial Services Industry living in the Midlands around Birmingham, Sutton Coldfield and Tamworth. After the passing of my wife Pat I decided in 2016 to move to Anglesey in North Wales, where in the solitude of coastal life my senses have developed in many spiritual ways, allowing me to do Philosophy, Mediumship and Healing. I am grateful for the life I have and hope the senses I have acquired will be used to further enhance the lives of others.

The Higher Level Of Consciousness

Well my beautiful beings of Love and Light, please understand as Universal energy integrates with the Earth's Consciousness there are bound to be physical and spiritual changes to us all. Although we are all at differing stages and dimensions the changes will be harder for some than others. We notice imbalances in our lives and our sleep patterns, please understand we are all being down-loaded with up to date programming to help in raising the earth's consciousness. Some will cast off their earthly physicality and operate on a more Universal plane, some will choose to spend time in the physical and meta-physical states and some will remain in the physical, it is all a matter to what degree of consciousness has been achieved. Many are still in the lower dimensions where as others have reached much higher levels of consciousness. The fact is we all need to work harder to achieve the levels needed to reach the higher levels of consciousness. For this is the way.

Blessings to you all.

Love and Light.

Vibrations

Well my beautiful beings of Love and Light as you may be aware the vibrations of the Universe are matched only by the vibrations of the Love and this is the vibrational levels that we as beings must aim to achieve. This is the scale of the task that lies ahead of each and every one of us. We owe it to our planet and ourselves to lift the earth's vibration of love to that of the other planets of the Universe. This should be realisable as we are universal beings, enjoy your journey.

For this is the way.

Blessings to you all.

Lighten The Load

Well my beautiful beings of Love and Light, life's journey is long and hard in itself, but it is made worse by the heavy burden we allow ourselves to carry with us. For goodness sake let go of yesterday's baggage and don't allow the past to drag you down. Rid yourselves of all the hate, ego and thoughts of revenge they are of no use to you and the people who you feel these things for probably don't even know. So fill your mind with thoughts of love, empathy and forgiveness, perhaps then your life's journey will be a lot easier and the pack on your back a lot lighter.

For this is the way.

Blessings to you all.

It's Not Your Role To Play

Well my beautiful beings of Love and Light prepare for the carnage that is to come, as the lower dimensions begin to awake from their sleep. Some will try and raise their conscious levels so be ready to assist them, others will choose to stay in the lower levels and look to repair the damage done by those who have enslaved the world over the millennia, who's structures are crumbling and falling apart. But now is the time for you to stay strong, watch and wait but resist the pull of the lower levels for it's not your role to play.

For this is the way.

Blessings to you all.

Rejoice The Time Has Come

Well my beautiful beings of Love and Light as we rise through the higher dimensions dear souls be aware of the changes to our physical and meta-physical states. The lightness, the imbalance as the earth's gravitational pull is weakened by the power of universal love and energy. These are not short term changes but everlasting forces meant to help release earth from the captivity and slavery. Rejoice the time has come.

For this is the way.

Blessings to you all.

A Message For David

Do not lose faith I am with you, I will always be with you although you do not see me, I see you, I hear you, I feel your despair, your loss. But stop, listen and you will hear me for I am never far from all of you. I will miss nothing for I am able to be with all of you, all of the time. Look for my signs that I send to you. Believe them for I stand beside you wherever you go. We may now exist on different planes of existence but our love will last forever.

Your Powers Are Awesome

Well my beautiful beings of Love and Light some mornings when you wake up for some reason you may feel grumpy, fed up, angry, depressed for no apparent reason, well take a good look at yourself no not in the mirror but inside yourself (find your inner being, your soul).Remember you are the creator of your own reality, so stop those negative thoughts and start to create the most exciting positive reality for yourself. Your powers are awesome, believe and remember it takes as much energy to create positivity as it does negativity. So it's a no brainer.

Blessings to you all.

Divine Right

Well my beautiful beings of Love and Light we are all divine beings and therefore have the divine right so start and exercise that right. Love, forgive, empathise and most of all be free to be able to do these things, do not allow the greedy, egoistic, hateful beings of earth take away your right, they are your Universal birth right.

For this is the way.

Blessings to you all.

Love And Consciousness

Well my beautiful beings of Love and Light the depth of your love is a clear indication to what levels of consciousness you have achieved. If you show unconditional love, empathy, forgiveness and understanding to yourself and fellow beings, then you exist on a high level of consciousness. If on the other hand you cannot, then you are still a work in progress (so to speak). On the other side of this if you are angry, lack understanding, cannot forgive or have empathy and do not love yourself or other fellow beings, then you are at a very low level of consciousness and need to take a long look into your inner self to find out what and who you really are.

For this is the way.

Blessings to you all.

Be Prepared

Well my beautiful beings of Love and Light no matter where we came from within the Universe, we came here to help to do a specific job, to help planet Earth develop. Many entities from various places in the Universe over the millennia have tried to distort, interfere and change the Earth's destiny. However these entities have in the main been thwarted with the help and assistance of friends from far off places. Yet for many centuries Earth and its beings have been held captive by various malevolent infestations but their time is fast coming to an end as their ways and structures collapse about them. They run to pre-arranged bolt holes (so to speak) but all will be in vain as Earth restores its balance of Love and Light. Beings from other planets have been standing by waiting for Earth to react and ask for their help. That time is now my friends so prepare for the greatness that awaits us.

For this is the way.

Blessings to you all.

Don't Lose Yourself

Well my beautiful beings of Love and Light it is so easy to give all your love, empathy and caring to all the people you meet on life's journey, that you can forget to give your love , empathy and caring to yourself. It is so easy for your pain to be lost amongst the pain of others and so at some point you need to take time to hold yourself closely and cherish the love and all the good that is you. For without being you it is not possible for all that love, empathy and caring to be given to others.

For this is the way.

Love and Light.

Blessings to you all.

The Journey

Well my beautiful beings of Love and Light, so as this earthly being is laid to rest his soul journeys onward toward eternal Love and Peace, for his passing is the beginning of his renewal and the next stage of his Universal existence. For his family that are left on the earthly plain take all of the love that you feel for him and wrap it around yourselves to hold, comfort and sustain you all at this sad time.

Love and Light.

Blessings to you all.

Your State Of BEING

Well my beautiful beings of Love and Light, when you begin to move from the darkness into the light, you begin to increase your consciousness. Consciousness is not a place or a thing it is a state of BEING, It is that point between here and there. It is not IS and it is not ISN'T (so to speak). It is just BEING and the higher you raise your conscious levels or BEING the closer to the Light you will be. If you breathe in and out BEING is that point where you are neither breathing in or out, that moment when you just BE, that moment when you are the Light, that moment when you come home, for you are a BEING of LIGHT.

For this is the way.

Love and Light.

Blessings to you all.

The Final Goal

Well my beautiful Beings of love and light why do you continue to search in the outer regions of consciousness, when the seeds of eternal love grow within you. These are the things you need to nurture to take you forward on your eternal journey. Money, greed, hatred and ego will be of no consequence to you as love purity empathy and forgiveness are the attributes you will need to find the light which will lead you to eternal existence, which is the goal we should all be aiming for.

For this is the way.

Love and Light.

Blessings to you all.

The Sins Of Our Fore Fathers

Well my beautiful beings of Love and Light, is it not enough? that we have had to carry all that pain, hurt and anguish for our lifetimes, that it will follow us when we pass over. Of course it is enough my dear souls, when we cross over we will be healed of all the pains, hurt and anguish, no more will Karma follow us in our new existences, as it has done through the centuries. The Golden Age of Enlightenment will mean the end of all of this. For because of this the sins of our fore fathers will no longer follow through to future generations.

For this is the way.

Love and Light.

Blessings to you all.

Arise From Your Sleep

Arise from your sleep my being of light.
Don't let the darkness prevent you from seeing
that the Age of Enlightenment is now upon you.
So wake up and see the golden dawn.
Arise from your sleep a new day is with you,
a new day, a new beginning for one and for all.
Believe in the oneness which has begun to surround you,
which joins and eternally bonds you.
Arise from your sleep there is no discrimination, hatred or racism, a new day has dawned and you cannot go back.
The road to ascension and eternal life is clear to see. The way ahead is there for you, so follow the light. So arise from your sleep beautiful soul for now is your time.

YOU the Truth

Well my beautiful Beings of Love and Light do not shy away from your truth, stay true to yourselves for it is your very essence, your energy and you reality, YOU. If you cannot be true to you, you have nothing for you are the truth, the reality and in Universal existence there is only YOU and YOU are the way.

For this is the way.

Blessings to you all.

Born Free

Dear Souls, the Unified Energy Field is not just a field of energy, it is consciousness itself (so to speak) and you are not just in it but everyone of us on planet Earth IS IT. Each one of us individually are self -creating pieces of consciousness creating our own realities, inter mingling with others, but none the less we are the same even though we may have different choices to make. We are beings of Love and Light and there for there should be no hatred, racism or any other form of negative energy between us, these are brought to us by the dark side and it is very destructive therefor we must all resist this and show our Light. The dark-side cannot win against the Light and so beautiful souls of planet Earth the time has now come to react with the Love and Light, send out the message to the dark side enough is enough and no more will the dark side have control over us and the Earth will be free from the slavery we currently endure. Do not let the fear they use on us distract you, be strong for without the fear the Dark-side have nothing. We will do this for the future generations of our children who will then be truly BORN FREE.

Love and Light.

As Above So Below

So, on the Earthly plain the perceived loss of this much loved family member leaves the family in a state of grief, though there is also a feeling of relief and gratitude that after a long and eventful life passed peacefully to "the other side". Where to meet her on arrival was her daughter Pat "Trisha" and her grandson Philip, who was without doubt very pleased and excited because his Nan had come to stay.

Love and Light.

(In Loving memory of Dorothy (Dot) Cheese who passed on 21/04/2015 at 05-30 hrs.)

I Am The Light

Last night climbed into my bed and switched off the light, immediately the bedroom filled with golden light. Beside me lay a baby girl yet to be born, a child destined to be a giver of life. Standing next to the bed was my wife Pat and son Philip, growing ever taller. Through my consciousness came orbs of golden light each one filling the room and then releasing millions of golden threads all over me and they kept coming, orb after orb I felt as though an Angel had wrapped his wings around and healed my troubled mind. For the last few weeks have not been easy. This morning I have woken from a beautiful sleep I feel relaxed and at peace within myself knowing that I am the Light.

For this is the way.

In Memory Of My Life's Love.
Rip Pat 3rd May 2011

Close your eyes my love, go to sleep for your earthly pain and existence draws to a close. Allow my love for you carry you forward to toward eternal peace. Think not of our parting but of our universal existence, holding us together for all eternity. It matters not that I am here and you are there resting eternally. This love that bonds us together is the glue, the cement of the universe, energy so strong that nothing can ever separate us, so close your eyes my love, go to sleep.

Love and Light.

I wrote this for me but truly it's for everyone who has gone through this traumatic time. Love and Light Alec. xxx

Who Are They?

Well my beautiful beings of love and light, who are these human beings who live amongst us doing daily routines the same as we do, who look like us, breathe the same air as us, however they are capable of travelling through time and space, are gifted in the skills of telepathy, seeing into the past, present and future. Who show great Love, Empathy and Forgiveness to their fellow man, who are sending out a message of world peace to all creeds and races bringing them together as one and why not we all share the same planet and breathe the same air. So who are they, these talented people, why, they are you and you and you, wake up my beautiful Beings of Light for your time has come.

Love and Light.

Blessings to you all.

One Of Life's Lessons

Well my beautiful beings of love and light, please understand the passing of a child either still born or at any earthly age is not necessarily only about the child but more about you. Ok, the soul of the child has signed a contract before coming here for this to happen, to help you as a person (or soul) to develop on your life's journey. Please understand this is not about the child, but you and how you cope with this very emotional state of events. Experiencing the Grief, working your way through all the stages of the Grief realising there is no set length of time this grieving will take, but never the less understanding that this event is going to mould how you will progress in your life and what and how you complete your life's journey. Rest assured this will have been a profound lesson of Love, Patience, self- control, anger management and self-healing throughout you journey and so for you, you will have experienced one of the many life's lessons.

For this is the way.

Blessings to you all.

Look For The Sting In The Tail

Well my beautiful beings of Love and Light, prepare yourselves for the changes that will come as the Forces of Dark begin to fall back. Increase your conscious levels to help cope with the changes. Believe that Mother Earth after many warnings is about to deliver justice on those who insist on ravaging her for their own personal gain. Retribution will be swift and brutal for those who follow the path of anger, ego and greed. Unfortunately many innocents will suffer as in any conflict and therefor you need to prepare and be ready to help those in need. Yes as always Love and Light will prevail but look out for the sting in the tail for the darkness will not give in easily and be aware that not all beings are what they may pertain to be. (wolves in sheep's clothing.) so to speak.

For this is the way.

Blessings to you all.

Don't Just Talk The Talk

Well my beautiful Beings of Love and Light, the truth is it is not enough to talk the talk so to speak, action speak louder than words. It is not enough to talk about Unconditional Love, Empathy and forgiveness we have to live it in every sense of our existences. It is no good saying one thing and doing something totally different. The Earth needs positivity now not just from one or two souls but from all of us, pulling together, going in the same direction. So create your own Love and Light and let it shine throughout the Universe. There is only one way to ascension and this is the way.

Love and Light.

Blessings to you all.

Patience

Well my beautiful beings of Love and Light do not be surprised that with the on- going flow of Universal, Cosmic and the Earth's energy mixing and blending there will be a huge change in the Love vibration within our planet. Be patient because of all the negative energy surrounding the Earth this process is taking much longer than was anticipated. Never the less the changes are steadily taking place. However beware of complacency as the dark side will not give up easily, they have too much to lose but lose they will and then they will find hiding places very hard to find as The Mother restructures what once was making there bolt holes disappear. With the increasing Love vibration their resistance and power will dissipate. My message is one of patience, do not get caught up in the upheavals of the lower vibration as they struggle to correct things, be aware and ready to act from your levels. Things do not happen overnight, but they will happen so be prepared. For this is the way.

Blessings to you all.

Trials and Tribulations

Well my beautiful Beings of Love and Light do not look back on the trials and tribulations of your past. Do not feel the need to carry them forward with you as you continue your spiritual journey of discovery. These are the things that have got you to where you are today, but are not needed as you go forth. They will only burden your soul and hold you back, so let them go, free yourselves and carry on with Love in your heart.

For this is the way.

Blessings to you all.

The Healing Tears

Well my beautiful Beings of Love and Light, please understand the pain of your loss can be immense and so your heart creates emotion within you which in turn brings tears to your eyes. Please do not fight the tears it is your hearts way of easing your burden and healing the pain. So do not be afraid to let your tears flow, let them heal your mind and soul.

For this is the way.

Blessings to you all.

Do not play the Game

Well my beautiful beings of Love and Light follow your dreams, your heart and the Love. Please do not get to journeys end to find out you played the game and didn't live your life as was intended. The game is to distract you from the true intention and purpose of your being. Remember it is much easier to play the game than it is to live your existence here doing the work that was intended for you. Follow the Light to achieve your goal of true unconditional Love, for this is the way for each and every one of us.

Blessings to you all.

An Eternal Flame

The pain isn't in your leaving or my letting you go.
For your time on earth had surely come.
The pain is in the knowing that you're closer than ever before.
I hear you, I feel you, I see you, but I can't touch you.
The pain isn't in the grief, or the anger.
The pain isn't in the feelings of guilt or disbelief.
The pain is in the knowing that I don't remember,
That we have been together so many times before.
The pain isn't in the emptiness you have left in my heart,
Or the loss of all our unfilled dreams we were to share.
No the pain is in the love and the knowing that we might have done so much more.
So until we do meet again, I will be helped by that love and the pain that goes with it.
So if you also believe this my love the flame will burn forever.
An eternal flame.

The way to Eternal Peace

Well my beautiful beings of Love and Light look within yourselves to find the love and happiness which is yours by right. Only by allowing other beings using negative energy can these things be taken from you. Resist negative people, live your lives with positive energy, forgiveness and unconditional love and the light that you follow will lead you to the Kingdom of Heaven and eternal peace.

For this is the way.

Blessings to you all.

The Threads Of Your Life's Journey

Well my beautiful Beings of Love and Light allow the threads of your life's journey be picked up by your consciousness. If you feel the need go into your past lives and discover the lessons you need to learn, journey into the future to help keep on your pathway. Allow your consciousness to show you that you are not what you pertain to be. You are a Cosmic Being held here on the Earth by your own free will (no one else's), to learn and for the Earth to benefit by your being here. Let your light shine brightly, others will see it and follow.

For this is the way.

Blessings to you all.

They Seek Your Light

Well my beautiful beings of Love and Light look for the peace and tranquillity within you at this time of super energy passing through you. Be aware of the changes that are happening to you sleeplessness, restlessness and uncertainty, these are all part of the shift that is occurring, let the Love and Light sustain you. The lower realms will begin to look for guidance from you but take care do not get embroiled in their activities, watch and be prepared it is your light they seek, you do not have to do anything at this time except let them see the light.

For this is the way.

Blessings to you all.

Teacher's Role

Well my beautiful Beings of Love and Light, please understand the teacher's role is to show you the Light. Your role as pupils is to choose whether you follow it. For this is the way.

Blessings to you all.

The Returning Home Of An Earth Angel

Well my beautiful Beings of Love and Light, let us celebrate as one of Earth's Angels returns to the Heavenly plain. She is a daughter, sister, mother, grandmother, niece and an inspiration to all of us but more than that she is Love and all of us at some time will have experienced that Love. Let us all rejoice that she is now free from all the Earthly pain as she continues her spiritual journey. As for us wrap that love she gave around us and let the warmth sustain and heal the pain, for without that Love there surely would be no pain. Remember her in our hearts and minds for she will be around us for all eternity.

Blessings to you all.

Remove Negative Energy From Your Life

Well my beautiful Beings of Love and Light, just because you have created a reality of positive-ness do not fall into the falsehood that all Beings do the same. Just because you are all Beings of Love some choose to create a negative existence of Ego, Jealousy, Hatred and a will to control others. Be wary and take yourselves away from these negative energies, remember you are all free spirits and as such you belong only to you for in reality there IS only YOU and all of these other things are all part of the illusion.

For this is the way.

Blessings to you all.

Be Of Pure Love

Well my beautiful Beings of Love and Light, I ask that you let the outside in and the inside out, blend and let the energy flow, mix with the Love that Universal energy is bringing to you. This is the way for you not necessarily for others at this time. To ascend your energy needs to be of Pure Love.

For this is the way.

Blessings to you all.

Earth's Universal Musicians

Well my beautiful Beings of Love and Light, let your heart resonate with the Universe, and let the beat of the Universe resonate with the beat of your heart, for the emotional ripple caused within you will become the music of the Universe and you, you will become at one with your heart and the Universe for music is the one thing that your emotions will resonate with and you will become one of Earth's universal musicians.

For this is the way.

Blessings to you all.

The Inner Sanctum

Well my beautiful Beings of Love and Light, sometimes we just need to put to one side our daily routines, sit quietly and listen to our Inner being and resonate with our soul, to find the inner peace we search for. This will not be found in the hustle and bustle of our daily lives, but in the peace and quiet of our inner sanctum. For this is the way.

Blessings to you all.

Inner Happiness

Well my beautiful Beings of love and light please recognise there are differing degrees of happiness. Some brought to you by others, some by giving in return happiness from your daily routines. But for true happiness only you can give by looking inside your inner being and finding your true self, who you really are (Oneness). Find the peace and tranquillity that lives within you and love yourself and then and only then will you be truly happy, for this comes from the heart and this is the way.

Blessings to you all.

I Am !! LOVE !!

Well my beautiful Beings of Love and Light it isn't why or how you feel, sense or touch who you are it is where you look. You do not have to search heaven and earth to find what you are looking for. Look within see your heart, feel your soul, inner being and you will not have to ask yourself "who am I" YOU will be able to say" I AM LOVE", and this is the way.

Blessings to you all.

Go With The Flow

Well my beautiful Beings of Love and Light, understand sometimes your inner self will tell you things your mind does not want to hear. Well listen up for your inner self/ heart knows more about you than you can possibly imagine, so instead of fighting with your conscience just listen and know then go with the flow for this is the way.

Blessings to you all.

Be Mind Full

Well my beautiful Beings of love and Light, do not allow your mind to instil negative thoughts into your heart. Thoughts of revenge, hatred, indifference and self- harm can only be self- destructive and will tarnish the beauty of the true love which flows within you. Go with the flow in your heart and let the love overcome all other thoughts that may distract you from your true self.

Blessings to you all.

Your Choices No One Else's

Well my beautiful beings of love and light I ask that you be aware of all the negative energy which surrounds you. Do not allow this energy to infiltrate your creation of positivity. Resonate with your heart and not your mind and this will assist you with the choices you have to make. These are your choices no one else's.

For this is the way.

Blessings to you all.

Our Soul's Journey

Well my beautiful beings of Love and Light, please give some thought to this. It is not your heart, eyes, ears, nose mouth or any other body parts that we need to sustain us whilst in our earthly role that we will take with us when we return to our spiritual home. No the one thing that will join us on our eternal journey will not be a physical body part but our soul, our inner being our very essence and within this will be the Love, Empathy, memory and the Light that we truly are and these are the things that we will need to help us as we follow our eternal path.

For this is the way.

Blessings to you all.

The Magic That Is Christmas

Well my beautiful beings of love and light, remember we are all part of one big family who want to experience the love, joy and forgiveness at this special time. So if you know someone who is down help them up, if you know someone who is hungry help to feed them and if you know someone who is in pain help to heal them in the true spirit of Christmas. For if we truly believe then we will all understand the MAGIC that is.

For this is the way.

Blessings to you all.

That Enormous Leap Of Faith

Well my beautiful beings of love and light, sometimes we need to take that enormous leap of faith into the unknown to enable us to believe. What comes easily for some may not be so easy for others. Trust your heart centre and your inner being (soul) to find your true self, your true purpose in life and go forward on your journey knowing that we are far more than we pertain to be.

For this is the way.

Blessings to you all.

Earth Angels

Well my beautiful beings of Love and Light please understand that Earth Angels come to you in many forms and guises. Some may be givers of their time and energy at whatever cost to themselves, others may be in the form of the needy or helpless who would ask you of your help, time, energy and perhaps money. They will give to you or ask something of you, please realise that these things are all a test of you, your character and how far you have progressed on your life's journey of learning. They will surely test your Love, Empathy and Will to Give and your willingness to forgive so in your daily routines be aware for they will visit you at any time and without prior warning. Many of you may well have already experienced such things.

For this is the way.

Blessings to you all.

Authenticity

Well my beautiful beings of Love and Light would you please recognise that to be authentic you need to realise that there is positive and negative energy in you existence. You need to create with positivity and not allow negative attitudes into your creations for this will surely dim the Light that emits from you.

For this is the way.

Blessings to you all.

Change In Direction

So my beautiful beings of Love and Light please understand that from time to time and particularly at this time of the year, the Universe will put different situations in front of you, it may be a place, a person or an event whichever this is a time of choices your choices. If you are undecided ask your inner self for a wrong choice can take you in a totally different direction to the one destiny intended. Believe that for you this is a time of change to what you have been and a correction to your life's journey, so go with what your heart and soul tells you to do, for in the majority of times change is for the better and the feeling in your soul is never wrong.

For this is the way.

Blessings to you all.

Total Love..................No Guarantees

Well my beautiful beings of Love and Light please try and understand sometimes to love is not enough, you may well have to add forgiveness, empathy, caring and understanding especially of you and your partner's needs. Total love is within all of us it is an integral part of our self -worth, but be aware that because you are able to give such love your partner may not, because it comes from within does not guarantee total love coming to you.

For this is the way.

Blessings to you all.

Love:- Lessons To Be Taught And Learned

Well my beautiful beings of love and light there are many lessons to be taught and learned when we broach the subject of love. I believe it is possible for each and every one of us to attain more than one real love in our lifetime. There was a man who lost his first real love through a lack of understanding of one another's needs. Then he lost his second love through his jealousy and the fear of losing her and ended up driving her away. His third real love and ultimate love was taken from him on the earthly plain through illness as she joined her son in the land of spirit, but because their love was total love their souls are for all eternity. The lesson is never give up in your search for total love, be forgiving, caring understanding, loving, trusting and believe and possibly you to will find that total love that we all search for and please remember that it is already deep inside our souls. However please do not have expectations of such love to come to you from others as we are all at different stages of progress.

For this is the way.

Blessings to you all.

The Healing Light

Well my beautiful beings of love and light it was nearly five years ago after the passing of my beloved Pat I wandered aimlessly in the grief and the darkness of my mind until I saw a pin prick of light far away in the distance. The closer I got the brighter the light became until I was completely immersed in it and parts of my being began to fall away from me memories, ego, and feelings of guilt until I stood there completely naked bared to my soul. As I moved forward further into the light I began to feel healed and began to notice other parts of me, love, compassion, empathy, forgiveness and understanding. The healing light moulding me into the being I was meant to be and the person you all know today, gone that man most people would have known and so from the depths of despair I found myself at last knowing who I truly was and being on the path I was meant to walk with feelings of hope, joy and happiness, continuing on my life's journey toward my destiny.

For this is the way.

Blessings to you all.

Seperation Of Space and Time

Well my beautiful beings of Love and Light please understand that throughout our journey there are times of great joy at the birth of our children and sadness at the passing of our true love. This is a time when family comes together as one with love for each other pulled by the grief of their loss, supporting caring and looking after each other through this very difficult time. However at some point there has to be a separation of space and time to allow the future development of everyone, this will not be an easy time but is essential for the future growth and development of the family.

For this is the way.

Blessings to you all.

Ripples In The Water

Well my beautiful beings of Love and Light can you understand that our lives our very existence is just like the sea, each happening we experience is just like ripples in the water. Sometimes a large wave may come and wash us away and we will have to start all over again, but for sure like the sea our existence is endless, we may not always end up on the same shoreline but for sure we will end up on a shoreline our destiny dictates.

For this is the way.

Blessings to you all.

You Are The Universe

Well my beautiful beings of Love and Light consider this, the depth of the Universe is equal to the depth of your mind. For you are the Universe and the Universe is you, as the universe is infinite so are you and only you can gauge the depth of you mind or the Universe. Please recognise yourself for the being you truly are.

For this is the way.

Blessings to you all.

Your Heart And Soul

So my beautiful beings of Love and Light please understand, the secret of true love is to resonate with both your soul and you heart, for true love can only be when both are one and you can only receive such love if your heart and soul are pure. We are all Light beings and only our human-nous can deny this love, once we have tasted the joy of such love we can never return to what we may have been.

For this is the way.

Blessings to you all.

Your Universal Self- Belief

Well my beautiful beings of Love and Light it is not enough to believe, that belief must come from your inner most self, from the very place that nothing or no one can put doubt into your mind. For it is from the centre of "YOUR" Universal Self and is Indestructible.

Blessings to you all.

You................The Source

Well my beautiful beings of Love and Light please realise that on your life's journey there is only you everything else is an illusion, along the path there will be people, events and places put before you and you will have choices to make. Ask your inner being which choices you should make for it is never wrong, these choices will determine your true destiny and the source that is truly you.

Love and Light.

The Real You

Well my beautiful beings of Love and Light please understand that all of your body parts are tangible things, a space suit helping to keep you here on earth, whilst your mind and soul are infinite, the real you. You are a universal being here with the express purpose of helping planet earth evolve to its true vibration. Beyond the earth many other such like beings are waiting for that time so that they too can help. So my beautiful beings patience, continue showing your light for others to see and for sure our time will come.

For this is the way.

Blessings to you all.

The Source Is Love

Well my beautiful beings of Love and Light, as we have spoken of many times before our lives are full of choices that we have to make, some easy and some more difficult. It may sometimes happen that for whatever reason a couple may decide to abort a child and the child returns to source and lives on and grows in the land of spirit. The spirit child will sometimes manifest itself in future children of the couple as they all belong in the same soul group and carry the same Genes, frequency and memory. The parents can see the image of their lost child within their family group. It is not uncommon to see this in photographs of past generations of the family, for instance a photograph of say their great grand-parents with a very similar appearance as themselves, for the people who have made these decisions no doubt will have spent years beating themselves up with feelings of guilt and misgiving. The time must come to forgive themselves for no one but themselves are hurting. The child who returned to source has grown and will love them, as the source, is Love.

Blessings to you all.

How Do You Mend A Broken Heart?

Well my beautiful beings of Love and Light, Earth Angels, Healers and Empaths, all gifted talented Beings capable of True Unconditional Love, Forgiveness, Empathy, Spiritual Healing, Psychic abilities, Terrestrial travel to the depths of the mind and the Universe I have but one question to ask of you on behalf of all beings who are suffering. !! How do you mend a broken heart!!

Blessings to you all.

Reach Out And Touch With Love

Well my beautiful beings of Love and Light, please understand it does not matter where you go or who you meet on your journey, if you travel with an open mind you will be joined by beautiful people full of you, for we truly are one so we must reach out and touch with LOVE AND RESPECT.

For this is the way.

Blessings to you all.

Multi-Dimensional Pathways

Well my beautiful beings of love and light please try and understand there are many pathways in your existence. Some plain to see, some hidden, others straight or twisting and turning and also crossroads these pathways are your destiny, your way home. Also remember you are a multi-dimensional being therefore these paths are with you at all levels of existence. You will meet other beings along the pathway but they are on their pathway not yours, some will be like ships that pass in the night whilst others like stars that will shine in your existence forever.

For this is the way.

Love and Light.

Be A Free Spirit

Well my beautiful beings of Love and Light, create your own reality and live it. Try not to be tempted into playing the game which is for the lower vibrations. Your role is to show your light for others to see and follow, which in turn will raise their consciousness and they too will be free. For this is the way.

Blessings to you all.

Love and Light.

Friendship

Well my beautiful beings of Love and Light, it is not uncommon for beings to form friendships with other beings, whom for one reason or another share the same path, this is not to say that they are on the same life journey as you are. However there will come a time when there must be a parting of the ways, do not be afraid to let go for this is the way and how it is meant to be. So enjoy the time learn and move on.

Blessings to you all.

Go With The Flow

Well my beautiful beings of love and light, when you're life seems to be in disarray and indecision look inside your inner being and find the silence that is within you, for within the silence you will find peace and the answers that you are looking for. Go with the flow, for once the universe recognises you're intentions it will flow with you and put in front of you people places and situations , take care and by using your intuition you will make the right choices which will lead to happiness, peace of mind and calm on your on going journey, whereas the wrong choices will leave you on the wrong path altogether.

Love and Light.

Blessings to you all.

Returning To Self

Well my beautiful beings of love and light please be aware that there may well come a time when things we naturally take for granted such as water, electricity, fuel and readily available supplies of food etc. are suddenly taken away from us either through natural disasters or other means. Please understand the earth is in a very delicate state at this time of its development, so it may well be prudent to start and become more self -sufficient and start to grow your own food and perhaps collect your own water. It may also in time be a good thing to try and form communes within your community so that you can help support each other, you might also consider bringing family closer as the means of travelling long distances may well disappear. There are clearly things that you can do now to help your situation in the future. There is no need for panic or to rush immediately into a total change but it will certainly be prudent to start living a much more independent form of existence and look more to self.

Love and light.

Blessings to you all.

Love And Everlasting Light

Well my beautiful beings of love and light, because you are reading this you know that you're a spiritual being having a human experience. You may well experience emotions such as jealousy, anger, hatred, greed and so on, these are traits of your human-nous. Please do not be disappointed by this react to it with love and understanding for they are all part of your learning curve on a journey leading you to love and everlasting light.

Blessings to you all.

One Energy One Love

Well my beautiful beings of love and light like so many other people we spend a lot of our time asking questions of others about who and what we are, what are we doing here on earth, when actually we should look inside and ask ourselves for no one else knows the answers. Within ourselves in the silence that is where we will find all the knowledge we seek. Of course this will not be possible without the belief, the belief that we are not what we pertain to be, for once we have seen the inner light all will be clear, that the answers we sought were there all the time. For some of us reading this we already know for we have the belief, for others it is all there for we are all one, one energy one love.

Blessings to you all.

A Time Of Change

Well my beautiful beings of love and light, many of us will know by now that 2016 is definitely a time of change. Many will feel as though they are being tossed by stormy seas others being pulled this way and that, not knowing quite what to do. Some however will follow their hearts, listen to their inner selves and go with the flow of the universal energy which is transforming us on our onward journey. ENJOY.

Love and light.

Blessings to you all.

The Price To Pay

Well my beautiful beings of love and light I ask you to think on this, if we are all spiritual universal beings who self -create our own realities, why is there so much hatred and pain on our planet. Perhaps as self- creators we all have a choice to do good or bad and perhaps some of us allow our human-nous to affect those choices instead of using our spiritual gifts. If all beings were to listen to their heart and choose to work from a loving place the earth would be a better for all of us to exist. My warning to those who choose to work from ego, hatred and with no empathy for their fellow beings, this is not the way to eternal life and you can look forward to a return journey to help you come to terms with who and what you truly are, a being of love and light.

Blessings to you all.

Working Together In Oneness

Well my beautiful beings of Love and Light, don't just look upon yourselves as one look at the whole universe as one. For surely we are all one, self- creating energy, positive and negative energy working as one to create the Love and Light to transform the whole world and it's vibration for the universe to see the earth coming together in oneness.

Love and Light.

Blessings to you all.

Lessons To Be Learned

Well my beautiful beings of Love and Light the earth as we know is being ruled by evil, greedy, egoistic people who are waging war on the weak, women and children. As new universal energy arrives into earth's energy field bringing love and peace to us and our vibrations of love rise to higher levels, these evil people will find a resistance to their wicked ways and destruction will fall upon them and their followers. Their life's journey will not lead to an on -going eternal existence, but more likely a return to the earth to learn the lessons of Love and Light.

For this is the way.

Blessings to you all.

Love And Light The Magic Words

Well my beautiful beings of Love and Light, please understand it is not for you to teach others spirituality for they already are spiritual beings. It is for you to show your light for them to follow and discover who and what they are and not what they pertain to be. None of this is rocket science it is so easy, Belief and Love are the magic words and once they have discovered these things the rest will fall into place.

Blessings to you all.

The Finding Of True Love

Well my beautiful beings of Love and Light, look beyond the quietness of your surroundings to the inner silence of your very being. Here you will find the True Love which is you for you are Love. For without recognising who and what you truly are you will not be able to find what you seek from others for you simply will not be able to see it within them, so before you start looking elsewhere for the Love, look within. For this is the way.

Love and Light.

Blessings to you all.

Anchor Yourselves To Your Inner Being

Well my beautiful beings of Love and Light as the universal energy sweeps over us and pulls us to and fro in all different directions we need to anchor ourselves securely within our inner self and go with the flow. This way you will remain grounded within yourself and all the changes and decisions that are to be forthcoming you will be able to make the right choices and remain on your life's journey, although during this time your vibration and consciousness will raise your abilities to cope will see you through.

Love and Light.

Blessings to you all.

A Different Level Of Consciousness

Well my beautiful beings of Love and Light you will understand that recently the earth's energy has received a massive boost of consciousness from the universe which has raised our vibration to a much higher level. The consequence of this is that we are much more aware of what is around us (so to speak). Whereas before we may have sub- consciously travelled within our own realms, we are now capable of reaching realms that were previously beyond our capabilities. This means connecting to our many multi- dimensions and you may well find beings from those existences visiting you,this is new and a direct result of our increased levels of love and vibration. Enjoy for we are indeed in a totally different level of consciousness and being.

Blessings to you all.

Giving And Receiving

Well my beautiful beings of Love and Light,that time of the year is once again upon us whereby we celebrate Christmas, the season of goodwill. Christmas holds many differing thoughts and reasons for being for each of us. But the one thing most of us believe is that it is a time for giving and receiving gifts so when you prepare your meal on Christmas day think of a loved one who has crossed over and lay a place at the table for them, for surely they are with us all the time and no doubt will be recalling those happy times when we were all together on the earth plane, or fill that place at the table with some-one less fortunate who for whatever reason find themselves alone at this time. Please understand that in your giving you are also receiving for your vibrational levels will increase by the love you have shown, not just for now but also for times past. For the earth to raise its vibration and become a much better place to be we must help each other by showing our light in a way others will see and begin to show their light and the universe will see the groundswell of love shining strong and bright from our beautiful planet.

For this is the way.

Blessings to you all.

In Loving Memory Of Mac Goldie. Rip

So for us who have been left behind we fall into a whole host of emotions caused by the love we had for Mac, who has now passed over. All the feelings of disbelief guilt, anger regret and the missing, all are part of the grief at our loss. As for Mac he has cast off his malfunctioning space suit which kept him here on earth and has returned to his spiritual home, a truth seeker who is now healed of his earthly experience and has now found out that all the things he wanted to believe whist on the earthly plain are true and he has now joined with his spiritual family to continue his eternal journey. We on the other hand will miss him, but also rejoice at his passing for he has achieved the purpose of his earthly journey, true love and the earth has been a better place for his being here.

Love and Light.

Suggestions From The Universe

Sometimes the universe will suggest moving from one path and show us a more direct one to take us to where we need to be. This may not always fit in with our perceived plan but it will be the way we are meant to go and no matter how much you resist you will always end up on the path meant for you. So be at one with you and go with the flow.

Love and light Alec.

She Is Gone

You can shed tears that she is gone
Or you can smile because she has lived.
You can close your eyes and pray that she'll come back
Or you can open your eyes and see all she's left.
Your heart can be empty because you can't see her
Or you can be full of the love you shared
You can turn your back on tomorrow and live yesterday
Or you can be happy for tomorrow because of yesterday.
You can remember her and only that she's gone
Or you can cherish her memory and let it live on.
You can cry and close your mind,
Be empty and turn back
Or you can do what she'd want:
Smile, open your eyes, love and go on.

David Harkins (1959)

These words were read out at a funeral in the West Midlands last week. They are so beautiful and profound, just take a moment to stop and wonder. Love and Light. Alec.

A Thought For Today: Act Of Self Destruction

From time to time humans come to the earth and because of circumstances which they cannot control, pain from loss or perceived loss, guilt or grief find themselves in a no man's land (so to speak). For them there are no foreseeable solutions to their problems and so by an act of self -destruction they leave the earthly plain. This is a time of pain and sorrow and the unanswered question of WHY from their family and friends who are left behind. As souls on this spiritual journey we must realise that this event was agreed to by them before they came to the earthly plain and so the day they returned to the higher realms was their day of destiny and their departure to the higher realms was pre planned.

Love and Light.

A Thought For Today: Universal Love

The universal word is love, so put your hands across your heart and love yourself as the true being of love that you are, because for sure you will be unable to give such love to others unless you LOVE YOU.

Love and Light.

Blessings to you all.

A Thought For Today: Emotions

As spiritual beings understanding we are all pieces of Universal energy positive and negative. Part of our human-nous are our emotions, these are our feelings promoted from the heart and will be as good or as bad as our attitude determines. So if you have negative feelings you will have negative emotions and conversely if you are positive your emotions will be positive and happy. The Universe says be positive be happy.

Love and Light.

Blessings to you all.

A Thought For Today: Ever Changing Universal Beings

The universe is saying to you “look upon your soul’s existence as the oceans and you are a mere pebble being tossed rolled, turned and polished by the ebb and flow of the ever changing tides, fashioning you into the being you truly are on this life’s path, an eternal ever changing, Universal Being of Love and Light.

Blessings to you all.

A Thought For Today: Transcending Beings

Well my fellow Beings you will understand that the cleansing of all your human emotional states as you begin to transcend to the next level of your existence. The Earth chakras that have been so powerful for you whilst in a state of ascension will be put to one side as your outer chakras come into play. Obviously this does not apply to all as many of you will opt to stay grounded on the earthly plain. Once again we will have choices to make, please understand once you have reached the level whereby you are transcending there can be no going back to your old state of existence. Most beings at this time may well stay in a state of ascension (vibration) and others will transcend into Universal Beings.

For this is the way.

Love and Light.

A Thought For Today: The Universe Says "Create The Perfect Home"

The universe says in your mind create a firm base. In your mind create a strong foundation to build upon. In your mind create a sound structure to protect you. In your mind create a home to dwell in where you will find peace, calm and tranquillity. Then you will have created the perfect home within your mind where you can just "BE" at one with the universe.

For this is the way.

Love and Light.

A Thought For Today: Finding Inner Peace

Lose yourselves in nature and natural surroundings to find the inner peace you crave for.

For this is the way.

Love and Light.

A Thought For Today: Relinquishing The Past

As universal energy enters the earth's consciousness and begins to cleanse our energy of the ego, greed and racist attitudes, be prepared for the uplift in your consciousness as this new energy will leave no stone unturned, so to speak. The effects will be felt in every walk of life. This will not be an easy time for us, not only does it mean you relinquishing the past but there will be others who do not want to let go of the ego, greed etc. because of the importance they place on these things. Little do they know that none of these things have any credence nor will they follow them through into eternal life, only love and forgiveness will do that.

For this is the way.

A Thought For Today: Learn The Lessons

Please understand no matter how hard and stony your journey may be your soul and consciousness will adapt and still grow and develop. Each hardship each stone are all part of your growth as a universal being. So take every experience, mistakes and regrets you may have and put them all behind you where they belong and move forward toward your destiny.

For this is the way.

A Thought For Today: The Enemy Within

I believe it is generally acknowledged that religion is a man- made form to restrict and control all of the earth's populace. We, our souls are beings of universal energy within an energy field called consciousness, in fact the reality is we are that consciousness, tiny pieces of self-creating energy known collectively as !! oneness !! So if it was not for interference from the enemy within, energies who want to divide us for their own ends we would all live as one…………………………………………….just saying.

For this is the way.

A Thought For Today: Nothing Stays The Same

As Universal energy within consciousness you are a self-creating Being, so you must expect things, events and other Beings on your pathway to change as they like you evolve although I realise most of us do not take readily to change usually due to the fear of the unknown. Be prepared, for nothing stays the same on this fast evolving journey.

For this is the way.

Love and Light.

A Thought For Today: Research Your Truths

Recently I have had thoughts and indecisions brought about by the concepts of others who believe differently to me due to the teaching and indoctrination they have received during their lifetime here on planet Earth. It is very difficult to know whether what you have been brought up to believe is true or false. So I ask that you try and look beyond the nine dots (so to speak), don't just put to one side something you are told go out and discover for yourself, research and find your truths for sometimes the truth will be a thousand miles away from your teachings.

For this is the way.

Love and Light.

A Thought For Today: Be the creator

Be the creator of your creations.
Not the creations of another creator.

Love and Light. Alec xx

A Thought For Today: Go With The Flow

Well my beautiful Beings of Love and Light, understand sometimes your inner self will tell you things your mind does not want to hear. Well listen up for your inner self/ heart knows more about you than you can possibly imagine, so instead of fighting with you conscience just listen and know then go with the flow for this is the way.

Blessings to you all.

A Thought For The Week: To Be Happy

To be happy be the heart and love of the Universe. For this is the way.

Love and light. Alec xx

A Thought For Today: Drifting emotions

If you find your emotions adrift in the ocean swells, find a piece of driftwood and ground yourself to the shoreline.

Love and Light. Alec xxx

A Thought For Today: Illusions Of Life

Beware of the illusions in life, for things aren't always what they appear to be.

For this is the way.

Love and light Alec x

A Thought For Today:
Effects Of The Seasons

It doesn't matter whatever the season; Spring, Summer, Autumn or Winter there is something about the sea shore that connects with the universe and your soul.

For this is the way.

Love and Light. Alec xx

The Christmas Visitor

If we can understand that the only difference between us and those who have passed to spirit is that we still have our "spacesuits" and theirs are cast to one side, redundant so to speak. So it follows that our memories of them and theirs of us will be more or less the same. For most of us our happiest memories are around Christmas time, a time of giving and good cheer, of course for family in spirit they too will share these times with us so it seems only right that during our Christmas festivities we set a place at out tables so they can join us as our very own special Christmas visitor. A light showing us the way.

Love and Light.

The Love Energy

You my beautiful beings are the brightest stars in the planet earth's night skies, so let your light burst forth and let the other beings from all across the Universe see the love energy that we all are.

For this is the way.

Love and Light.

Our Origins………… The Reality

Although generally we class ourselves as human beings due to the indoctrination we have been put through over the millennia. It is however far more likely our ancestors came from regions of the universe far from planet Earth and it is most likely most of us descend from those beings, so it follows that our ancestors were more likely to be Aliens, ET'S or Star Beings for example. Our energy is electrical frequency and our origins can be determined by Dowsing that energy, as each type of being has a different frequency it can therefore be determined where our origins lie. By using dowsing it is also possible to recognise any inappropriate entities within your energy field, these can be removed and the space created by their removal can be filled by inviting in more positive energy. Some of us may be surprised by this but there will be others who will just know. All depends where you are on your journey.

For this is the way.

Love and Light.

What Is Love?

Some say love is passion, belief in each other, understanding and forgiveness. Some say love is the emotions, feelings that flow through your soul when you meet your matching pair. Some say love is the joy, happiness, total fulfilment in the belonging. Some say love can be painful, hurtful and disillusioning. I say by putting all of these things together you have unconditional love, available to all but given by so few of us, however if you have received such love then you are truly blessed. We may all have differing views on this but what I do know is that if you are the recipient of such love then you will discover inner happiness the like of which you will have never experienced before. The quirky thing is just because you love someone unconditionally it does not guarantee that they can love you unconditionally in return because we all love differently.

For this is the way.

Love and light.

The True Meaning Of Life

So what is the true meaning of life, is it your true worth? Is it your true value to others? Is it the thing that makes you tick? Is it a gift that you have acquired since birth or were born with? No the true meaning of life is none of these things it is how much you are loved. It may not always fit comfortably with you, but to be loved is everything for we are love.

Love and light.

Creation

Your dreams, your aspirations should be your creation not someone elses. For the end of your journey is not a representation of their lives but of yours. So many of us follow others like sheep without realising we are living another's dream, so be at the front of your creations and just BE.

For this is the way.

Love and Light.

We Are All One With The Universe

Moonbeams dancing on the water, energy's of the moon light going with the ebb and flow of the tides. The oceans cleansing the earth's memory as they come together, brief moments in time where the earth, sea and the universe mix as one. ONENESS.

For this is the way.

Love and Light.

Who's Responsibility Is It?

As creators of our own realities, If another being comes to you in anger or ego this is not about you or what you may or may not have done. It is about them for they are the creators of their reality and therefore they are responsible for their actions.

For this is the way.

Love and light.

Windows Of Opportunity

Windows of opportunity are there for all of us to see, however only those who are awake will actually see them. Choices will be put before you, they are yours to make, use your intuition as a wrong choice will leave you on the wrong path. Don't despair on your day of destiny you will be exactly where you were meant to be, though your journey may have been more difficult because of those wrong choices you made earlier.

For this is the way.

Love and Light.

Just BE

Search for the sea of tranquillity within your soul. Find the peace and calm in your mind, know that the silence is golden. From within all of these things find your true self, your inner being and live in the now. So just BE.

For this is the way.

Love and Light.

Changes On The Road To Ascension

As waves of Universal energy flows into and blends with the Earth's energy you will suffer pain skeletal, muscular, nausea and headaches, some to a greater degree than others depending on the amount of change necessary. Many are ready and prepared for what is to come, so fear not those who need to change will be ready, however there will be many who are reluctant or not wanting to change so be it, we all have choices to make but as earth's consciousness rises they will be the ones who do not avail themselves of the help made open to them, not in their human-nous but in their spiritual being. Many will ascend to the higher consciousness having let go of their past, some will stay in this consciousness to help those who change their mind to ascend by increasing their vibration, once we have moved to the higher vibration there can be no going back.

Love and Light.

The Pathfinders

Because we are the Pathfinders the road to ascension will be harder as we travel through time and places few humans have ever been before ,meeting Beings from other dimensions, Beings of many shapes and forms of life unknown to us now but whom we will become aquainted with. Our minds and thoughts will be stretched further than we could ever imagine as we let go of the past and flow toward our final destination/Eternal life.

The Earth's Energy Field

Please try and understand that the air that we breathe is an energy field, known at first as the Zero Point energy field and then in December 2015 the reactor in Switzerland discovered it at that time I channelled the statement "We have allowed your scientists to make an important discovery however they do not appreciate exactly what they have discovered. It is a gateway to the universe allowing us to travel through our consciousness to wherever we want to go including back and forward in time. The field as we know it today is consciousness itself and we don't exist in it WE are it for we are all individual pieces of self -creating, positive and negative energy. So beware if you think negative thoughts, negative things will happen around you , whereas if you think positive thoughts you will have a positive existence, so try to be positive at all times. So consciousness is made up of tiny pieces of energy, all of us in the entire world so we are all one there should be no racism, greed or ego the collective of this is "ONENESS". We should all strive to help each other succeed for if one fails we all fail and vice versa if we all succeed the earth will be a much better place for everyone.

So within the consciousness we have the past, present and the future, our medium friends use their energy and vibration to look into the past to bring us contact with our loved ones who have passed to the spirit world, which of course they are not a million miles away as they share the consciousness with us though be it at a higher vibrational level. Psychics on the other hand do the same but look into the future to see visions of things and happenings to come. Healers use the energy within consciousness to heal and relax us, all of these are within our reach if we BELIEVE of course at this moment there are many who do not believe and our responsibility is to show them our spiritual light. Their responsibility is to see and follow their spiritual path, but of course we all have the choices to make.

Love and Light.

So Who And What Are We

So who and what are we Earth beings, Human beings, Cosmic beings or Universal being. In reality I believe we are not what we pertain to be, our human-nous is our spacesuit so to speak which allows our true being to survive on the earth. Which is why when we finish our time on earth we leave the space suit behind to be disposed of as surplice to requirement and we take our soul (spirit) Frequency and memory with us intangible things to use on our onward journey of ascension through the different vibrations and dimensions. It is a journey of transcendence toward eternal life and to re- creating our next reality's within the soul groups that we belong in

Love and Light.

The Effects Of Universal Energy

At this moment in time Earth's energy is being infiltrated by Universal energy. As Earth's energy is far from being pure eg. greed, ego, hatred racism etc. the Universal energy needs to blend with it to help purify our energy. Ok as beings of energy this must have some effects on us for eg. At this time we may experience tiredness, aches and pains in our bones and muscles and of course high pitched ringing in our ears. Now this symptom is not new to us, the medical world puts this down to Tinnitus of which they say has no cure but if we accept that we are beings of energy, does it not make sense that we will hear other energy remember this has been going on since time began. These are symptons which will effect some of us more than others depending to a degree on their vibrational levels. This cleansing of the Earth's energy is essential in raising the Earth's vibration to higher levels where pure love, purity and forgiveness will play a much larger part in our existence.

Love and Light.

A Guide To Understanding Your Spirituality: Who Is God?

Ok so 'who is God', a question often posed with so many differing views. Let me put forward another view, a spiritualist view for you to ponder over. If we can accept as previously stated that we are self- creating Universal beings, whereby we as individual pieces of Universal energy create our own realities the good the bad and the indifferent, then it seems to me that it is infinitely better to create a positive reality rather than a negative one. So back to the question who is God? Well if God is the creator and we are the creator, then God is us and we are God and if we all form the greater consciousness then we are all one God.

Love and Light.

A Guide To Understanding Your Spirituality: Universal Beings Of Love

Ok so we're saying universal energy is purity, well to me that means pure love, unconditional love therefore if we are these small pieces of universal energy then it follows that each and every one of us is love, unconditional love. So where does the jealousy, greed, hatred racism and lack of forgiveness come from. Well just because we're universal beings we are also earth's consciousness and unfortunately the earth's energy isn't pure which is why these flaws in us exist. So relax let the two energy's blend into one and we will become what we truly are beings of love and light.

For this is the way.

Vibration, Consciousness And Transcendency

At this moment in the Earth's development its vibration is at a very low level which is why Ego, Greed, Hatred, Racism etc. is common place. This is not as it is meant to be and the responsibility for raising this vibration is ours, the people of Earth. To do this we all personally have to raise our vibration through love and laughter, by doing this will also serve our consciousness and each and every one of us will rise through the levels to a point of transcendency whereby we will leave our human-nous behind and transcend into the Universal beings we are meant to be. Please understand none of this can be if we fail to relinquish things we hold on to as normal, for the lies we have been fed for thousands of years are beginning to have no credence or meaning for us. The thing to remember and understand is the choice of whether you remain in the 3rd dimension or go forward to the 5th dimension is yours and yours alone.

Love and Light.

A Guide To Understanding Your Spirituality: Walk The Walk

One of the things I have found about spirituality is that it's not enough to talk the talk you have to walk the walk. In other words it is ok to call yourself spiritual but to work from positions of ego, hate, racism, selfishness and being unforgiving does not do it, forget those things, put them all behind you and work through your heart with love, caring and forgiveness no matter what. There are plenty of beings on earth who prefer negativity rather than a positive attitude. Be the Light for others to follow they in turn will shine their Light and so it will go on and the whole universe will see Earth as the purist, brightest planet.

Love and Light.

A Guide To Understanding Your Spirituality: Expectations

Ok so let's take a look at one of our human failings. Generally we love and expect love in return, un-conditional love has no bounds or expectation. Expectation is the worst thing that we put into our relationships, it constricts and prevents proper development, un-conditional love allows freedom of will, growth and individual choice. Let your relationships flow and benefit from a happy existence. He who expects gets nothing.

For this is the way.

Love and Light.

A Guide To Understanding Your Spirituality: Who Are We?

Let us not forget who and what we are, beings capable of unconditional love, empathy, caring and forgiveness but also capable of selfishness, ego, deceitfulness and hatred. It is the ability to harness these things and bring forward all the positive attributions to the foremost parts of our mind. For we have the choice to be either side of our being and it is for us to be the former, to have unconditional love and show it, not only to the people close to us, but to others also. To have empathy and to feel and share someone else's pain. To care for others as you would care for yourself and to forgive for there is no greater love than to forgive someone who has hurt you. So if we do these things, the darker side of us will not be able to come through and destroy us.

For this is the way.

Love and Light.

Aguide To Understanding You Spirituality: Creation, Consciousness And Love

Each and every one of us is the Creator. Each and every one of us is Consciousness. Each and every one of us is Love. The problem we have is in the believing, over the millennia we have been instructed, taught and conned by society to think as lesser beings and lower conscious beings. Our human-nous has got in the way of what we really are. We are not slaves to a system of greedy, egoistic people. We are free spirits with great gifts (though many of us have forgotten how to use them). We are capable of unconditional love. We all have intuition (gut feeling). All we have to do is raise our conscious level high enough for these things to happen.

For this is the way.

A Guide To Understanding Your Spirituality: Look Within Yourself

Well I feel now is a perfect time for all of us to stop what we're doing and look within ourselves and ask our inner-being is it right that hatred, ego, greed, and tyranny should play such a large part in our existence. As caretakers of the earth would the planet not be better if love, empathy and caring for each were to be at the fore-front of our lives. We all know in our hearts that the earth is in a desperate situation and now is the time for all of us to rise up as one to ignite the light of consciousness and let the universe see that we are on the way back and that the people of the earth do care. If every-one on this planet were to light one candle of hope and peace, the flame would be seen through-out the universe. We do not have to do this physically, but by raising our conscious levels just a little, it will have the same effect.

For this is the way.

Love and Light.

A Guide To Understanding Your Spirituality: Peace On Earth

The aim of all of us should be to achieve Peace on Earth and this can be achieved when mind and consciousness come together, Inner- peace, when body, mind and consciousness come together and unconditional love empathy and caring come together. Without this, ego, anger and greed prosper and we fail to look after each other and so it is with the earth, there cannot be peace on earth until we raise our consciousness and mind, and start loving and sharing with each other, no matter what, for we are one.
Without each other we cannot survive as peoples or as a planet.

For this is the way.

GOD's way.

A Guide To Understanding Your Spirituality: Life

Sometimes and more often than not, the realities we create for ourselves clashes with the realities created by others. A mum loses a daughter or a son, this is her reality the passing of the child was its reality. The mum must now create a new reality, by increasing her consciousness and spirituality. Her child's day here is done, and it must begin again, for its day has yet to be.

For this is the way.

A Guide To Understanding Your Spirituality: Free Spirits

Right then let's take a look from a different perspective. The spirit world has a soul, memory, consciousness, frequency and of course love we also have a soul, memory, consciousness, frequency and of course we have love. However we have something else, our bodies, space suit which allows us to function on the planet Earth and our human-nous. The spirit world is free to go wherever and whenever it so desires, it can be in more than one place at any time because there are no restrictions hence the term Free Spirit. We on the other hand because of our human-nous are restricted and controlled by our bodies, by religion, by political abuse and enslavement by the system. This has been the case for millennium after millennium but this is not how it was meant to be, both worlds are the same energy field Earth's consciousness only in different vibration and dimensions and as the love from Universal energy infiltrates the Earth's energy it will clean out all the hatred, greed and ego that exists and we will all feel the benefits of the change in the Earth's vibration. It's not rocket science but it is the way it is meant to be.

Love and Light.

A Guide To Understanding Your Spirituality: The Real Reality

Ok try to see things for what they really are, for surely they are not always what they seem to be. Look beyond the obvious, the truth may well be something totally different. We perceive things to be as we have been taught by others. Find out for yourselves the true reality. Search your mind, consciousness, inner being and your soul for the truth lies within. Peace of mind, inner serenity is the way to total living, of being in balance with the universe and yourself.

For this is the way.

Love and Light.

A Guide To Understanding Your Spirituality: What's It All About?

Alright then so what is all of this about,spirituality, is it just about the spirit world and family and friends who have crossed over. Of course it's not although that is an important part. No, it's about unconditional love, purity, forgiveness, empathy and consciousness, all of these things coming together to save the earth from absolute and total disaster. We don't have to look far to see how we are in a steep descent into the abyss, being driven there by ego, greed, revenge and hatred. It will not stop unless the peoples of the earth stand together and say, enough is enough, no more. Let common sense pre-vale, let the love, empathy and purity shine through from us all. It is in us all, but we need a groundswell of earth's people to rise and put a stop to it, and then and only then will we have an earth as it should be. As was intended by the creator.

For this is the way.

Love and Light.

A Guide To Understanding Your Spirituality

Be true to YOU, for there is only YOU. Everything else is the reality of YOU.

For this is the way.

Love and Light.

A Guide To Understanding Your Spirituality

Create purity, unconditional love, empathy, oneness and light in your reality and for sure you will find the kingdom of heaven and everlasting peace. Not easy, but to ascend you will need all of these things.

For this is the way.

Love and Light.

A Guide To Understanding Your Spirituality: We Are What We Are

Oneness, what is… is, inner being, Phrases that we know well that tell us what and who we are, beings who reside on earth, earthlings, or are we universal beings who through our consciousness allows us to travel to the far ends of the universe. Perhaps casting off our mortal coil means something totally different to what we previously perceived. That it is our density our human nous that keeps us here with our feet firmly on the ground, when actually we were meant to go where ever and whenever we please or choose, a free spirit so to speak. Do not accept your human nous as you perceive it, step out and find the real you, that person, being you thought you might be and maybe just maybe you will see that you are.

For it's the way.

Love and Light.

Be Mindful

Please be aware of your mind, of what you think you are, therefore if you think positive things, positive things will happen. Conversely think negative thoughts and negative things will happen in other words your mind is your most powerful gift and your thoughts are creating your very reality. So use your mind to create a better lifestyle and a better way of living for yourself. This is about Inner peace, happiness and the very essence of what you are. Think of what you want from life, write it down, picture it and tell others what your aims and intentions are then go about positively achieving your goals. Become all of the things you want to be by using positive energy and your thoughts will realise a healthy reality. Remember if you think you can, you can.

For this is the way.

Love and Light.

Your Responsibility

You are responsible for you, if you want to know something ask your inner self, if you want to take action use your intuition, your gut feeling. Follow your heart go with the flow for in truth there is only you and it is your responsibility.

Love and Light.

What is Love?

Some say love is passion, belief in each other, understanding and forgiveness. Some say love is the emotions, feelings that flow through your soul when you meet your matching pair. Some say love is the joy, happiness, total fulfilment in the belonging. Some say love can be painful, hurtful and disillusioning. I say by putting all of these things together you have unconditional love, available to all but taken up by so few of us, however if you have received such love then you are truly blessed. We may all have differing views on this but what I do know is that if you are the recipient of such love then you will discover inner happiness the like of which you will have never experienced before. The quirky thing is just because you love someone unconditionally it does not guarantee that they can love you unconditionally because we all love differently.

For this is the way.

Love and Light.

* 9 7 8 1 9 1 2 4 0 0 4 0 9 *

BV - #0001 - 100220 - C20 - 210/148/8 - CC - 9781912400409